Divagations

Holiday 2024

The Angela Thirkell Society
of North America

Publication Title: *Divagations: Holiday 2024*
Issued: December 2024
Statement of Frequency: two times each year
Issue Number: 2-2024
Authorized Organization's Name and Address:
Angela Thirkell Society of North America
P.O. Box 80133
Lansing, MI 48908-0133
barsetshireATS@gmail.com

Original Drawings: Deborah Conn
Cover Design: Diane Smook
(cover photograph of ʻŌhiʻa Lehua flower by Susan Verell)
Editor: Susan Verell

TABLE OF CONTENTS

SOCIETY SECTION 1

Letter to the Editor 2

From the Chair 4

From the Vice Chair & Editor 5

From the Secretary 6

From the Treasurer 6

From the Agent for Service 8

New Members Report 9

Publications and Books Report 10

Holiday Gifts 13

National Meeting Possibility 17

Member Zoom Meeting 18

Renewal Time 19

FEATURE ARTICLES AND NEWS 20

Life, Love, & the Pleasures of Literature in Barsetshire .21

Summer Half Reflections 25

Foreigners in Barsetshire: An Introduction 35

Dues Reminder 41

Lydia and Rose and Shakespeare 42

Modestine and Other Donkeys 44

Married Couples Crossword 48

Sightings 49

Tidbits and Glimpses and Sightings 52

Crossword Puzzle Key 54

Angela Thirkell Titles 55

Contacts 56

SOCIETY SECTION

"Sir Robert agreed, and they cut the flowers and Anne put them in water and then it was time to change for dinner..."

---*Peace Breaks Out* – page 47 (Moyer Bell edition)

Letter to the Editor

To start this new feature in Divagations, *I asked UK's Journal editor Gill Watson to start us off with our first letter to the editor. I hope this letter is a preview of an upcoming article by Gill, and I support her encouraging Society members to explore the writings of Denis Mackail. I also hope that this letter will encourage all Society members to write with questions or ideas related to our Society and Angela Thirkell.*

The Polish American writer, Czeslaw Milosz, wrote, "When a writer is born into a family, the family is finished." However, rather than "finished," the Mackail family is illuminated for us by having two popular writers in one generation.

When I was looking for the models for Angela Thirkell's fictional dogs I didn't need to look far–Rudyard Kipling, J. M. Barrie, and her brother, Denis, were all serial dog owners–and it was through reading his *Life with Topsy* that I discovered Denis Mackail. Before long, I needed a new bookcase.

The animosity between Angela and Denis has been well reported, yet if you read their books, you see there are similarities in style and attitude that should surely have made them friends. But that's families for you, and the similarities can be what drives siblings apart.

I want to encourage ATSNA members who haven't done so before to look at Denis Mackail's memoirs, for the light they cast onto his and Angela's childhood and social circle. Without Denis's autobiographical *Life with Topsy* (1942), or his essay collections *Ho! or, How It All Strikes Me* (1944) and *Where am I? or A Stranger Here Myself* (1948) I wouldn't know that on Boxing Day at Rottingdean, the Ridsdales had a tradition of bowling oranges on the green at the local children; that Angela once told Denis their father's office was a hole in the nursery cork flooring (which he accepted at once, after all, "Angela Knows Best") or that he and Angela once "blew up" a French nurse using a chemistry set, "But there was no malice in this."

Denis Mackail seems to have suffered the same malaise and insecurity that affected his uncle Philip Burne-Jones and Georgiana's brother, Harry Macdonald, but I find Denis warm, funny, and unpretentious. I enjoy his reflections on childhood, on life during World War II, and on himself and his shortcomings, but especially the family history that doesn't appear in *Three Houses*.

From Gill Watson

From the Chair
Penelope Fritzer

As we approach the turn of the year, I am happy to report that the Society is in good shape: our membership is holding, we held our first member Zoom meeting and plan others in the future. We are still looking into a possible in-person meeting, although I have not heard back from many members showing interest in that, so we shall see this year what the responses are from both venues and members.

As always, we thank those who do so much of the work, including Susan Verell (*Divagations* editor and vice-chair), Melanie Osterman (treasurer), Suzanne Williams (secretary), Barbara Houlton (agent of service in California), Susannah Smith (website manager), Norma Munson (new members), Jerri Chase (publications and books curator), Diane Smook (*Divagations* covers), Deborah Conn (artwork), John Childrey (academic coordinator), and Tom Johnson (public relations). Many thanks, also, to those who contribute articles to *Divagations* and/or donations and/or gift memberships. And, of course, to all those members who help to spread the word on Angela Thirkell and her Barsetshire series in various ways (dragooning one's friends and relatives?).

We are able now to get back on the schedule of mailing the yearly UK *Journal,* which comes out in the summer, to our members in the fall, after some years of needing to mail it in the spring (as this past spring and fall), so the plan is that you will received it in the fall going forward. This means you now will get the UK *Journal* in the same year it was originally published, so can enjoy it in a timely fashion.

I wish each of you Happy Holidays, Merry Christmas, and Happy New Year, and hope to hear from you with written contributions to *Divagations.*

From the Vice Chair & Editor
Susan Verell

This issue of *Divagations* completes our publications for the members of the Angela Thirkell Society of North America for 2024. I certainly enjoyed bringing them to you and want to thank all those who provided help along the way. Your skills and generosity are both greatly appreciated. Our officers stepped up to the plate with submissions as well as asking others to do the same. If you have an idea for an article, please take the plunge and write it! It had been many years since I had written an article for *Divagations,* and I wrote one for this issue about one of my favorite Thirkell animals. It was easier and more enjoyable than I expected.

Moving forward, in 2025, you will receive *Divagations* in April, the UK *Journal* in September, and the holiday *Divagations* in December. If you are working on an Angela Thirkell-focused publication, please contact Chair Penelope Fritzer and me.

A special, heartfelt thanks to this issue's contributors. A shout-out, too, to John Childrey for his work in procuring Verlyn Klinkenborg's article on Angela Thirkell. Thank you again to all our members for your support, encouragement, and for paying your dues, too. You are appreciated.

From the Secretary
Suzanne Williams

This has been a fun and interesting year as recording secretary of the Angela Thirkell Society of North America. We have moved forward into the 21st Century using the technical tools available to us that Angela Thirkell could never have imagined. Think how an email thread between Lucy Marling Adams and Emmy Graham Grantly discussing cows might have read!

The Zoom software program is a particularly useful tool. The board of directors has met on Zoom to discuss issues important to the Angela Thirkell Society, and earlier this summer we held the first Zoom meeting with a few volunteer members. It was a success as participants shared their ideas about Angela Thirkell and our Society.

I continue to look for members who would be willing to contribute content to the Angela Thirkell Society of North America. I will be making direct contact with members to solicit their ideas and how they would like to contribute. Short and pithy observations about the novels and characters are always fun to read.

From the Treasurer
Melanie Osterman

As always, nothing is interesting about bookkeeping. That is, of course, for normal people.

But to a bookkeeper, you get a different slant on the topic. I look forward to the monthly bank statement and balancing the account. It is very gratifying to take the balance for the beginning of the month, take off the checks, add in the deposits, and find that you exactly match the bank statement. Or even better, to find that the bank made a mistake!!! And then take your proof (you always save the records) to the bank and show them their error. Granted it doesn't happen often, but it does happen.

Beyond that, I have been working on indexing all the old *Bulletins / Divagations*. It is so interesting to find things that were brought forward in the past that I have never heard about. The back issues are filled with gems: reports on meetings and presentations, library collections, Mrs. Thirkell's history and that of her family, relationships she had with people of note, as well as sightings, puzzles, and recipes. It allows me, and eventually you, to read back issues and revisit great pieces from the past.

Dues Reminder

Please don't forget to pay your Angela Thirkell Society of North America dues and maybe give a gift membership.

Please send $15 for each membership to treasurer Melanie Osterman at Angela Thirkell Society, PO Box 80133, Lansing, MI 48908-0133.

Please include your email address, phone number, and address in your renewal envelope

From the Agent for Service
Barbara Houlton

Although I consider myself primarily the historian (along with Edith Jeude), I also have a corporate title, and that is "Agent for Service," meaning "Agent for Service for the State of California Corporation, the Angela Thirkell Society of North America." This means when the California secretary of state, the federal government's IRS, or the California Franchise Tax Board have something to say to us, I hear from them, and the California government wants to write to me at a California address. Overall, this is not usually a friendly holiday greeting, and we are grateful to Susan Scanlon in the past and now Melanie Osterman, as treasurers, for making sure California's questions are answered, as they are almost always about money. What these government agencies want to know is how much money we have collected from people and what we do with it.

This is usually easy for us, as we spend almost all of the Society's money on publications, some postage, and various filings that these agencies require us to do. Because we are so small, all our activities are done by volunteers.

And so, from someone who has been with the Society since 1996, when I read Hermione Lee's article in the *New Yorker* and ordered one of the books from the "libery," which proved to be *August Folly*, here I am now, wishing you a happy holiday and urging you to send in your renewal now for a tax deduction for any 2024 donations.

New Members Report
Norma Munson

The number of new members for January through October 2024 was four. They're located in Maine, Ohio, Maryland, and Florida. As usual, after I receive the names and postal information from the treasurer, I put together a new member packet containing a welcome letter, a map of Barsetshire, information from Jerri Chase about ordering used Thirkell novels from her to fill out members' collections, a couple of past Thirkell Society publications, and a Thirkell bookmark. New this year is my having the current *Divigations* sent to the new member directly from Amazon. The Amazon costs and the postal costs for the packets are turned in to the treasurer at the end of the year for reimbursement. As I write, a new bookmark project is in the works.

It was interesting earlier this year to participate in a Zoom meeting with some members and some of the Thirkell board. It was delightful to see and hear the enthusiasm of the new and veteran members, and I hope we get to know each other better either via their contributions to *Divigations* or via another Zoom sometime.

My very best wishes to all Thirkell fans in 2025 as we continue to discover new delights with each reading and re-reading of the novels of our favorite author.

Publications and Books Report
Jerri Chase

Thinking about my contributions to the Angela Thirkell Society of North America, I see by checking the back of *Divagations* that I am listed as "Publications and Books." I think of myself as having several distinct duties.

A major duty is "book redistribution." When members, and on occasion non-members, contact the Angela Thirkell Society looking for new homes for books by, and occasionally about, Angela Thirkell, I have been the person to whom the books are sent. Therefore, Dan and I have to come up with ways to store the books to (1) make it possible to find out what we have, (2) keep them as safe as possible from damage and (3) make it possible to locate a requested book to send to members. Remember: any member of the Angela Thirkell Society of North America can request books by Angela Thirkell with the only costs of shipping and packaging. Media rate postage in the US is quite inexpensive on the whole, but the postage costs to other countries make this benefit most useful to those who live in the US, although on occasion I have mailed books to a US address that a member who lived in Canada or the UK was going to be visiting soon, so that they could then pick up the books and take them home! A few years ago, a generous member of the Society gave a large donation to cover the cost of postage, but that has been running very low. Most of Thirkell's books are available to members through this process in one format or another, sometimes in multiple formats. Any member interested should please send me your wish list!

Another duty I fill using the books that have been donated to the Angela Thirkell Society is to build up collections of

Thirkell's books that are suitable to be donated to universities or other research libraries, or in some cases books that can be donated to libraries that want to have a circulating collection or sets of several copies of the same title for the use of book clubs. Members who have contacts at libraries that might be interested can contact me and/or other members of the Society's board.

Then there is my custody of publications ABOUT Thirkell and/or her works.

One example of this is *Going to Barsetshire*, a wonderful reference work (one of the few reference books I know that is fun to just sit and read, and very beautiful also) written by Cynthia Snowden. When sales of the book caused Cynthia to take the book "out of print," the remaining copies were sent to the Angela Thirkell Society of North America. There are still some copies left, but when these are gone, the normal used book market will be the only way to acquire a copy. So, if any member is interested, please let me know. The Angela Thirkell Society also has a few copies left of *Angela Thirkell: Portrait of a Lady Novelist* by Margot Strickland, again for the costs of postage and packaging.

I also have in stock a supply of various Society publications, including but not limited to: *Bulletins, Divagations, Journals* and other special publications of the Society. Some are what was left in the Society's files after copies were sent to members and some have been included when members or the families of deceased members sent the Society donations of books. When duplicate copies are available, I also distribute these to interested members.

I also have been sent over the years various collections of what I will call the Society's "archives," including at least one copy of each of the Society publications, photo albums, and memorabilia including but not limited to tea towels, mugs, CDs, shirts, calendars and much more. I have been trying to become organized enough to get copies of early Society publications to treasurer Melanie Osterman, who has been working on indexing all of the *Bulletins* and *Divagations*!

I think this just about covers the position. A two-drawer filing cabinet, a library book cart, some bookshelves, some cardboard boxes, and five plastic storage bins contain this wealth of resources and Society history. Where this will go and how to get it there when the time comes that Dan and I must downsize may become a question for some future Angela Thirkell Society of North America board.

Holiday Gifts

The topic for this issue of Divagations *is: If you could give a holiday gift to one or more of the characters in Barsetshire, what would you give him or her and why? These can be practical gifts, luxuries, or maybe a skill that you feel he or she could use.*

From Melanie Osterman:

If I wanted to give a gift to someone in Barsetshire, I would give Laura Morland a package of "real" steel hairpins. The tortoise shell ones may be pretty, but they don't hold.

Happy Christmas to Clarissa
From Her Friend Suzanne Wiliams:

If there's one activity fraught with peril it is choosing Christmas gifts. You search store aisles, holiday arts & crafts fairs, or perhaps your own re-gift closet shelf for that perfect something to match with that perfect someone. The last few years I conceded the Christmas shopping spirit to Amazon. As my favorite celebrity chef would say, "How easy is that?" So long as the credit card and bank are on speaking terms, pretty darn easy.

Or there's always the cop-out: gift cards.

What would I give to which Barsetshire character? Now that's something to ruminate.

I did have a rather blasphemous thought: Present Lord Pomfret a case of a "5-hour Energy" drink. He's always run-down and tired, in good times as well as bad. He needs a jolt of something. I wanted to fist-bump Lady Agnes Graham when she brought Lord Pomfret up short by telling him His Majesty also came into his responsibilities sideways and His Majesty's were a lot heavier than Lord Pomfret's. Hand Lord Pomfret that energy drink.

So, if I had to pick someone truly in need, to whom would I bestow a Christmas gift? My gift goes to Clarissa Graham, and it is not something wrapped and ribboned: Purpose.

Clarissa Graham is probably the most disappointing of all Mrs. Thirkell's Barsetshire characters. She does not develop Clarissa into a young woman of her time. From the very start, Clarissa comes across as a spoiled brat, a condition she never outgrows until finally she marries that shallow schoolmaster Charles Belton. She is the least sympathetic of Mrs. Thirkell's core Barsetshire characters. Probably the only more obnoxious character is Frances Harvey (the Dreadful Dowager being more comic than obnoxious).

Clarissa is the intelligent, attractive, second daughter of a loving, secure middle-class family. She is not as boisterous or single-minded as her sister Emmy, and Clarissa is not as precocious as her younger sister Edith. The Clarissa we get to know creates flower arrangements, retouches the gilt on woodwork, and paints watercolors. I think these activities and interests manifest an artistic talent. She has an eye for beauty and design. However, Mrs. Thirkell never allows Clarissa to develop her talents. After Clarissa takes her "good second" in math from college she doesn't go on to work at any job, much less a profession. That is also something Mrs. Thirkell is loath to do: none of her woman characters are allowed an intellectual or active professional life. Her women do useful county jobs and then settle down to their real purposes of becoming wives and mothers. I found it odd that one evening Martin Leslie muses that none of his "women folk" were well-read.

So why do I want to gift Clarissa a purpose? Because I believe Clarissa does have a brain and talent. What she lacks is direction. Sir Robert is absent and lets his wife Lady Graham deal with the girls. She neither discourages nor encourages Clarissa. Instead, she is merely puzzled by Clarissa's wanting to study math and become a draughtsman for Sam Adams' works.

My take is that Clarissa's purpose should have been to develop her artistic talents. She might have focused on interior design; or, perhaps, she might have studied art and become an artist herself or a gallery owner. An even wilder speculation is that she might have taken advantage of knowing Jessica Dean and become a set designer for Aubrey Clover's very clever and popular plays.

However, Mrs. Thirkell never gives Clarissa the same passion for art and beauty as Emmy has for cow-mindedness. Clarissa is not allowed a talent or purpose beyond the domestic realm. This is too, too bad my dears, because with a bit of tweaking Clarissa's story might have been fun.

A Gift for Mr. Downing from Sara Bowen:

One aches to make Punshions a more comfortable place for both Harold Downing and Ianthe Pemberton. It can be done, as the nurse trio proved after Ianthe's death. But Ianthe wasn't a person whose boundaries you want to cross, so I will leave her to her own choices.

What is it about Harold Downing that makes people want to take care of him? I confess that his obsession (and Ianthe's) with the *Biographical Dictionary of Provence (BDP)* does remind me of Casaubon's obsession in *Middlemarch* with *The Key to All Mythologies*. But we meet people where they are and realize that our friends and family wonder about our odd literary obsessions.

15

So now, the best gift I can wish for Harold Downing and his new bride, Poppy Turner, is that Harold's lectures at Porter University are such a success that he is gifted even more support by Walden Concord Porter – not just a lecture series, but a well-endowed chair of Provencal studies. The endowment comes with funds for eager young research assistants who enter all the entries for the BDP into up-to-date databases on new computers and eagerly search for more entries to move the BDP past Mas-Moult to final publication online and in hardcover (supported by Walden Porter and his university press).

Unlike George Eliot's Casaubon, Mr. Downing would then see the fruit of his labors in his lifetime and add that satisfaction to his creature comforts in Northridge and Texas with Poppy. The completed BDP would be dedicated to Ianthe Pemberton and Walden Concord Porter, the odd couple that made its completion possible.

From Jerri Chase:

Somehow, I can't think of Christmastime in Barsetshire without thinking of Gunner, Modestine, Sylvia, and all my other animal friends (the ones named come from *August Folly* and *High Rising* in particular). I hope that they all get some delightful special treats to feast upon, and the cats get to climb into empty gift boxes, the dogs get to lie on top of the crumpled wrapping paper, and Modestine isn't too often pressed into service to carry some Barsetshire youngster to the inn in the Nativity play!

My other gift also isn't a physical gift: I want to ensure that kind Kate Carter, who had been Kate Keith, gets to host a wonderful Christmas gathering, which she with her love of being domestic would enjoy very much indeed. All of her siblings (Lydia, Robert, and Colin) and their spouses and children would attend. I think perhaps Anne and Robin

Dale and their three children would come also, as Robin's parents are both gone, and I think Anne's parents are busy in London with something political. The children would enjoy playing together, the men would all end up talking Southbridge School shop, and the women would talk about their children. The real Christmas gift would be the fact that Kate was able to secure the assistance of some of the Bunce and Thatcher women to do ALL of the washing up (Kate may love to be domestic and to be in charge of the feasting, but I don't think even this most domestic of Thirkell's creation actually enjoys the cleaning up afterwards!). The Christmas gift to the Bunce and Thatcher families is some very high-quality left-over food for their Boxing Day dinners and I am sure that the handsome payments for the domestic assistance will help pay for the family's Christmas presents. And the holiday gift to me would be that I would be an extra guest, enjoying meeting all of these lovely people in person!

National Meeting Possibility

You were mailed a letter in October regarding the tentative plans for an Angela Thirkell Society of North America in-person meeting in Wilmington, Delaware, April 25-27, 2025. If you haven't already reached out to Secretary Suzanne Williams (see her contact information on the last page of this issue) with your response, please do so today. The hotel rate is $149 per night, and the other meeting costs (including two breakfasts and two dinners) are also $149. Thanks for responding by December 15 regarding your interest in attending, as plans must be confirmed with the hotel very soon.

Member Zoom Meeting

In June, the Angela Thirkell Society of North America experimented. The newest subscribers were invited to a Zoom meeting with the board of directors. The hypothesis was (1) to gauge if there is any interest in the idea of holding meetings in this way, and (2) to see if this would be successful. The answer to both questions was YES; the meeting was a great success. Ten people participated–it is so nice to be able to put faces to names.

Board members went into the meeting with the understanding that if there were any of those great awkward silences that tend to proliferate among strangers, the board members were to chime in to fill the gap. After all, the point was to hear from the new people, and not talk much ourselves. With introductions all around, Susan Verell, our vice chair/editor, threw out a question, and we were off to the races. The silence never came, and people were vying to respond. No fillers were required. The conversation was detailed and informative, and the ideas were creative and insightful. There was representation by someone currently in the field of higher education, someone who was an archivist, and a member whose parents held NYC teas for Angela Thirkell Society members in the past. These participants brought their interests in Angela Thirkell to the forefront for discussion and provided interesting avenues to pursue in the future.

All in all, it was a lovely way to spend an hour on a hot Sunday afternoon–discussing our favorite person and her writings.

Renewal Time

The Angela Thirkell Society is an organization where membership is renewed on the calendar year. Dues are due by January 1, 2025. The Society has maintained dues at $15 a year for what seems like forever. Still, as you can imagine, it is possible only because people are always generous, enabling us to meet our costs from our current income. Our generous donors enable us to publish a book when we have one. If you have ever contemplated writing a book – there is no fixed length –contact Susan Verell, Editor/ Publications Chair, and Penelope Fritzer, Society Chair. They would certainly welcome a proposal from you. Society members are both readers and writers, with specialized knowledge as background. Please consider the Society as a vehicle for your Thirkell-related writing.

Another Dues Reminder

Please don't forget to pay your Angela Thirkell Society of North America dues and maybe give a gift membership.

Please send $15 for each membership to treasurer Melanie Osterman at Angela Thirkell Society, PO Box 80133, Lansing, MI 48908-0133.

Please include your email address, phone number, and address in your renewal envelope

FEATURE ARTICLES
AND NEWS

"I say, Colin, let's have a picnic on Sunday up the river.   If it goes on being as hot as this it'll be ripping."

--*Summer Half*, page 99 (Hogarth Press edition)

Life, Love, & the Pleasures of Literature in Barsetshire

Taking Comfort in the novels of Angela Thirkell

By Verlyn Klinkenborg

Professor Klinkenborg currently teaches at Yale University. He has published articles in The New Yorker, Harper's Magazine, Esquire, National Geographic, Mother Jones, *and* The New York Times. *His books include* The Rural Life, Making Hay, The Last Fine Time, *and* Timothy, Or Notes of an Abject Reptile. *He served on the editorial board of* The New York Times *for sixteen years and was a recipient of a Guggenheim fellowship.*

The weather has been cold, the snow deep, the long, dark evenings perfect for holing up with a book. In the past few weeks, I've read nine of Angela Thirkell's Barsetshire novels. I expect to keep on going right through all twenty-nine of them, and I may go back to the beginning when I am done and start over again. This is a confession of sorts. When I first came upon Thirkell, many years ago, she seemed like a diverting minor writer – a comic realist, of sorts, describing a world whose fictional boundaries might be P. G. Wodehouse and Dorothy Sayers. "Minor" seems too slight a word to me now for the purveyor of such major pleasures.

I don't remember exactly when I first came across the novels of Angela Thirkell. It was probably on a day when I set off with high purpose into the book stacks of a university library – only to be distracted, as always, and find myself wandering down aisles I had no intention of visiting. Perhaps I came across some reference that aptly called Thirkell a minor Jane Austen. Or I may have been led directly to Thirkell while reading Trollope because she

21

borrows and extends the geography of Barsetshire, Trollope's fictional English county. In any case, I bought my first copy of Thirkell – a paperback of *Wild Strawberries* – in October 1981.

Thirkell wrote nearly a novel a year between 1933 and her death in 1961, all set in the fictional English county of Barsetshire – a landscape borrowed from Trollope, who was himself the prolific author of novels that once seemed more minor than they do now. Unlike Trollope, Thirkell is uninterested in money, politics, and ecclesiastical power. She is even uninterested in denominational squabbles. Many readers would say she is interested in love because each of her novels ends with an engagement – the formal sign that hers is in a comic universe. But love is not what interests her. It is just the device that frames her books, that brings them to a point.

One of Thirkell's characters is Laura Morland, an author of mysteries – one a year – set in the fashion world. "Not but what they are all the same," Mrs. Morland explains, "because my publisher says that pays better." Thirkell's novels are the same, too. If you cut only the scenes that take place during tea, half of Thirkell would be missing. I'd like to say her countryside becomes more intricate, novel by novel, but it doesn't. The war darkens it, and so does England's dire recovery from the war. But her continuing characters continue just as they've always done. Mrs. Brandon wins the heart of every man she sees. Mrs. Morland is forever losing her tortoise-shell hairpins. A tough, young heroine – determined and dutiful – is always falling at last into the arms of a sensible man, who is often her elder by more than a few years.

What interests Thirkell is people talking, and the nonsense they talk. It makes no difference who. It might be the chaotic English of a Mixo-Lydian refugee in a novel set during the war or the inane chatter of the beautiful Rose Fairweather, whose favorite adjectives are "dispiriting" and "shattering," though she has never been dispirited or shattered. Mrs. Morland is famous for her snipe-flight monologues, which are echoed and embroidered and, finally, trumped by her effusive friend, the biographer George Knox. It is Knox, who, in a fit of illness in the first of these Barsetshire novels, says to Mrs. Morland, "Even Wordsworth was more interesting than I am at this moment."

These are novels full of what might be called applied literature, whole lifetimes of shared reading welling up allusively in conversation. The reader hears the constant sound of familiar authors passing back and forth behind the scenes, like servants heading from the kitchen to the dining room in great houses like Marling Hall and Beliers Priory. And yet the talk is wonderful because it is simply neighborhood gossip. The war encroaches on Barsetshire, but the gossip continues, against a broader, grimmer backdrop.

Thirkell has often been called nostalgic because she is describing a kind of life – English country life – that was vanishing even as her books were appearing. Yet there is nothing nostalgic or sentimental in her tone. She is brusque, efficient, judgmental, and also somehow, tolerant, for without her tolerance these stories would never get off the ground. If she pokes fun at Miss Hampton and Miss Bent, a gay couple living in one of the Barsetshire villages, it is nothing compared to the fun they poke at everyone around them. For every Mr. Bissell – a schoolmaster fond of referencing the "Cappitleist" – there is a Mrs. Bissell, who is the soul of efficient goodness. Thirkell's characters are never profound, but they do not know it. We are never in doubt of a happy ending.

That is one reason to love Thirkell – the simple reassure-ances these books offer. But there are many other reasons, too. Somehow, as you read her, you can feel the world around you poking and prodding at her text. How do those May-December marriages – contracted with a single kiss–actually work out in the end? Is there really no crime? No outbursts of repressed rage? Is genteel poverty always resolved by a fortunate marriage?   In the end, these questions matter no more than the question of Thirkell's literary stature. You read her, laughing, and want to do your best to protect her characters from any reality but their own.

Please consider writing for our new Letters to the Editor column. Ask a question, make a statement, offer advice, anything that might improve the understanding of Angela Thirkell and her writings. Submissions for the next issue should be submitted before February 15,

Summer Half Reflections: Looking into the Heart of a Schoolmaster

By Mary Faraci

Florida Atlantic University Professor Emeritus Mary Faraci continues to make notable contributions to Divagations.

Recommended for Angela Thirkell's "observational skills and wit," *Summer Half* has been summarized as a comic story about a boys' school with introductions to Lydia, for example, and other stories we will see in later novels (Temple). While Thirkell entertains us with pranks, quarrels, and accidents during school life, she celebrates the vocation of the schoolmaster dedicated to keeping great books alive.

As the daughter of J.W. Mackail, an Oxford professor of poetry and a former secretary of the Board of Education, Thirkell defended her father's policy (Faraci 89) against movements of "State education" (*Love among the Ruins* 15). She worries about keeping great literature alive "till such time as state education has turned out enough illiterates ... and universal dullness buries all" (Introduction, *The Warden* xviii). In a typescript for "Is Fiction History?" a lecture she gave at Yale and Columbia, she remarks on the fear of losing freedom "to choose our own reading," saying, "It seems to me quite likely that in the Literature Manuals of 2049—when we shall all go to state nursery schools the day we are born and probably never be allowed to leave school till we are about 45 and never allowed to choose our own reading—that the 19th C will be called The Age of the Novel" (Faraci 90).

Grateful for her arts and humanities background, Thirkell designs *Summer Half* as a refresher course on Horace's rule to "instruct and delight," Virgil's faith in "Love conquers all," and, from Cardinal Newman's *The Idea of a University*, "Knowledge is its own reward." To bring us back to school, Thirkell creates a world of school-life duties, curriculum conversations, and lasting friendships. She throws uniforms on us: "a grey silk blouse, a blue gym tunic, and a blue blazer with brass buttons" (12); she drops names of Roman and English writers: Horace, Virgil, Shakespeare, Milton, and more (26; 143); she inserts school-life terminology: "Mixed Fifth" (53), "Lower Fourth" (221), "Junior Classics" and more (31). Our new friend, Lydia, makes passionate speeches about poets and how to teach Shakespeare: "If Shakespeare had wanted it paraphrased, he would have done it himself" (142).

From the first sentence of *Summer Half*, Thirkell drops readers into a review of schoolmasters. Only the onset of "complete senility" frees Mr. Birkett to replace the "licensed old imposter," Mr. Bradford (7). Early in the novel, Thirkell describes the "[l]oathsome visions of novels on school life" that scared Colin Keith: "falling in love with the headmaster's wife, nourishing unwholesome passions for fair-haired youths, carrying on feuds, intrigues, vendettas with other masters," and more (8). Her Barsetshire readers, as early as 1937, knew that *Summer Half* would be different from the familiar "novels on school life." Trusting her characters, Thirkell lets them entertain us with stories about great and less great schoolmasters. She warns against hiring "from somewhere where they teach teaching" (34). With gratitude for her literary upbringing, Thirkell celebrates schoolmasters who dismiss talk of "the galling servitude of schools and the brutal tyranny of the schoolboys" (22-23) as they accept the call to move their students through the arts and humanities. Her characters wonder about the "'something. I don't know what it is'" in the schoolmasters' vocation (95). The lawyer Noel Merton observes, "'I suppose schoolmastering is a kind of lay priesthood'" (95). The novel notes that schoolmasters are sometimes mocked for their lack of common sense. For example, a student mocks Mr. Winter for being engaged to the headmaster's daughter: "'Mr. Winter thinks he is all up to date...about What is being Kept from the Public, but as for knowing anything about life—'" (140).

Imagining a schoolmaster for the hero of *Summer Half*, Thirkell names Everard Carter after Colonel Markham Everard, the hero of *Woodstock*, a novel by Sir Walter Scott. She puts the novel in two scenes in ways that compare to how marketers place brand name products in movies: "Whether the audience realizes it or not, the product's visual placement is intended to capture the viewer's attention and influence their future buying decisions" (Shopify Staffers). Persuading readers to pick up *Woodstock*, Thirkell carefully places it in scenes featuring Rose Birkett, "a ravishing creature" (39): "Under Rose's window, Geraldine was reading *Woodstock*, which was her holiday task with Rose's bath sponge by her side" (183). Thirkell puts *Woodstock* in Geraldine's hands next to the bath sponge that Rose (imagining that her fiancée Philip Winter has been unfaithful and, at the same time, furious that her parents are encouraging her to break the engagement) has just thrown across the room and out of the window. Later in *Summer Half*, Geraldine happens to be reading *Woodstock* in the break-up scene of the engaged couple. When Philip asks Geraldine to let them be alone, "Geraldine said that she didn't see what they had to say to each other, but in any case, she had to finish the fourth chapter of *Woodstock*, a book which she freely characterized as mouldy" (232).

Thirkell praises Sir Walter Scott in her fiction and nonfiction for his imaginative, but persuasive approach to representing history (Faraci 26). For the instruction and delight of her reader, who is moved to pick up *Woodstock*, despite Geraldine's review, Thirkell offers Scott's historical novel about the escape of King Charles II. Adam Roberts summarizes his impressions of the novel in his notebook series in 2022: "The novel is saying that sexual exploitation and gratification is the 'truth' of love, and yet nonetheless is telling a love story, plotting out a narrative of devotion, honour and selfless love eventually rewarded." The heroes, Colonel Markham Everard and Mistress Alice Lee, face impossible obstacles to their future together: Alice is in love with Markham, a Cromwell supporter; and Alice's father, a Royalist, is against the union.

Recognized for writing remarkable conversations for historical figures, Scott imagines a clumsy argument that the vain King Charles II, disguised as a page, notorious for his "12 illegitimate children by various mistresses" ("Charles") would have made to Alice to be his mistress. An excerpt follows:

> "It is your king—it is Charles Stewart who speaks to you! —he can confer duchies, and if beauty can merit them, it is that of Alice Lee…. Know then, simple girl," said the King, "that in accepting my proffered affection and protection, you break through no law either of virtue or morality. Those who are born to royalty are deprived of many of the comforts of private life—chiefly that which is, perhaps, the dearest and most precious, the power of choosing their own mates for life….Society has commiseration, therefore, towards us, and binds our unwilling and often unhappy wedlocks with chains of a lighter and more easy character than those which fetter other men….And know, besides, that in the lands to which I would lead the loveliest of her sex, other laws obtain, which remove from such ties even the slightest show of scandal….So that Alice Lee,

may, in all respects, become real and lawful wife of Charles Stewart, except that their private union gives her no title to be Queen of England" (Ch. 26).

Apparently unschooled in matters of classical rhetoric about appealing to one's audience, the king feels sorry for himself, "deprived of many of the comforts of private life." Alice, caught in an awkward meeting with her king, redefines ambition to make a respectful argument as his supporter, not his mistress: "'My ambition,'" said Alice, "'will be sufficiently gratified to see Charles king, without aiming to share either his dignity in public, or his wealth and regal luxury in private'" (Ch. 26). Throughout the long exchange, Alice's superior rhetorical skills remind one of those of Jane Austen's Elizabeth Bennet responding to the condescending proposal of Mr. Collins (105-09).

As if honoring the 16th century English martyr, Blessed Everald (Everard) Hanse, Scott's Colonel Markham Everard, Alice's true love, distinguishes himself as a hero at every turn. Early in the novel he pledges to fast, "This day shall I not taste food" (Ch. 17), as an act of gratitude to God when Alice and her father can return to their home, Woodstock. When Colonel Everard hears reports of the threats to Alice by the disguised Charles, he confronts him: "'[Y]ou have rewarded the hospitality of the family by meditating the most deadly wound to their honour'" (Ch. 24). The exchange is so angry it almost leads to a duel. As a string of the couple's brave actions impress the king, by the end of the novel, the restored King Charles II makes a plea to Alice's father to accept the Colonel. A patriotic subject, and grateful for the King's support, Colonel Everard weighs carefully the choices before the nation: "submitting to Cromwell's subsequent domination, rather as that which was the lesser evil, than as that of a government which he regarded as legal…. [He became] of the opinion, which was now generally prevalent in the nation, that a settled government could not be obtained without the recall of the banished family" (Ch. 38).

By naming the housemaster Everard Carter, Thirkell compares the extraordinary merits of Scott's hero with the heroic work of schoolmasters. Thirkell drops a hint about connecting the hero of *Summer Half* with the hero of *Woodstock* even before she puts the book in Geraldine's hands. Rewriting history, Thirkell borrows Cromwell from *Woodstock* for her love triangle in a scene where Lydia, sharing her high school assignments with Noel Merton, asks him: "'I say, do you hate Cromwell?'" Noel replies promptly: "'Loathe him'" (26). The Scott reader would recall that Alice's beloved Colonel Markham Everard, who considered the disguised Charles II as a rival, was a Cromwell supporter. Likewise, Everard Carter worries that Noel Merton is his rival for Kate. Eventually, readers meet Mr. Carter, "A man of about thirty-five, with fair hair and a thin, amused face, came into the room" (45). The Barsetshire hero makes a great first impression, "so wise, so skilled in the great subject of boys" (48). Thirkell puts her hero's skills to the test alongside appealing characters. There is the Classical Master, the Scottish Mr. Lorimer (perhaps a tribute by Thirkell for the Scottish painter, John Henry Lorimer, who died in 1936). With fond admiration, Thirkell describes Mr. Lorimer as "the middle-aged man with a gait and appearance of a tortoise and an uncanny gift for forcing his pupils into scholarships" (67). There is also his bright student, Percy Hacker, and his pet chameleon, formerly named Greta Garbo, now named Gibbon after the famous historian.

Readers are treated to a scene of heroic schoolmasters at work. After Hacker had let the tub overflow and left a lamp to catch on fire, Mr. Carter manages to weave a witty Latin joke into the scolding of the Classics student at the top of his class: "'You can't even tell a plain narrative of what happened. I'd better ask Mr. Lorimer to put you back onto Caesar. He would have given, at once, a clear and concise account of what had occurred, in *oratio obliqua*'" (66). Speaking later to Mr. Lorimer, the housemaster does not hold back: "The ensuing interview began in that a pitched battle between Senior Classics and Housemastering.... Mr. Carter pointed out that the classics appeared to be no preparation for life, as they did not, as far as he could see, even train a boy to think. Any child from an elementary school would, he said, have been able to give a clearer account of what had occurred than the head of the Classical Sixth." As the scene moves ahead, our schoolmasters show that they really are heroes: "They then both lost interest in Hacker" and shared a glass of sherry. The scene cannot close before paying tribute to each man: "'How I loathe boys and their ways,'" said Mr. Lorimer who...took promising boys to his home in Scotland every holidays." "'About mid-term I could kill every boy in my house with joy,'" said Mr. Carter, who liked being a housemaster more than anything in the world, and usually enlivened the tedium of the holidays by taking boys to Finland, or Mt. Athos" (66-67).

Two-thirds of the way into the novel, it is fitting that, in the company of Mr. Carter and Colin Keith, who has decided to return to law, Mr. Lorimer, "into his fourth glass of port," delivers a bold profession of faith in his work: "'Obscure as the schoolmaster's life may seem, depressed, degraded, we bear the torch for each new generation, we follow the gleam.'" He adds, "'Carter, though his whole span of life is no longer than my [35] years of work, has the holy flame'" (168-69). Who better to endorse Thirkell's hero, named after Sir Walter Scott's hero, than Scotland's Mr. Lorimer?

The housemaster hero of *Summer Half* advances through the Barsetshire series to become a headmaster and the head of a family so beloved by Thirkell that she names the

Carter's daughter Angela. When the family attends the Merton luncheon in the later novel, *Love at All Ages*, Thirkell notes, "All three children were good-looking and intelligent, as might have been expected, and also very well brought up" (LAA 167). At that same luncheon, Thirkell reminds readers of Everard Carter's *Woodstock* connection, when Mr. Carter, Noel Merton, and other guests admit their attraction to the dramatic takeover pulpit scene in Woodstock (173).

It is sad for all when Mr. Lorimer dies while visiting his home in Scotland. In the final scene with Hacker, Kate, and Mr. Carter, who is celebrating his engagement to Kate, Hacker congratulates the couple and then continues, "'And please, sir, I've got something that I think would please Mr. Lorimer very much. I got some black stuff from Nanny, and she lined Gibbon's cage with it for mourning, and I think sir, he's really turning black'" (252). On the word black, with love and respect for Mr. Lorimer, *Summer Half* ends.

Always frank about making "a living," Thirkell would say that her ideal reader is the one who buys her books (Strickland 150). Perhaps, also, she expected the *Summer Half* reader to have read *Woodstock*. A 2022 appreciation of Sir Walter Scott's works regrets that "These days, Scott's writing has fallen out of fashion thanks in part to the sheer length of the novels...but [even] the best does suffer from slow pacing" (Cook). That said, I know at least one happy Thirkell reader who keeps Scott novels on her "nightstand" ("What").

Works Cited

Austen, Jane. *Pride and Prejudice*. Oxford, 1988.

"Charles II of England." *Wikipedia*. Wikimedia Foundation, Inc. 28 June 2024. http://en.wikipedia.org/wiki/Charles II of England. Accessed 10 July 2024.

Cook. Daniel. "Walter Scott at 250: So much more than a great historical novelist." 21 June 2021. https://theconversation.com/walter-scott-at-250-so-much-more-than-a-great-historical-novelist-162638. Accessed 8 July 2024.

"Everald (Everard) Hanse." *Catholic Online/Saints & Angels*. 31 July 2024. https://en.wikipedia.org/wiki/Everald_Hanse . Accessed 7 August 2024.

Faraci, Mary. *The Many Faces and Voices of Angela Thirkell: A Literary Examination of the Brotherton Collection*. The Angela Thirkell Society of North America, 2013.

Horace. "He who instruction and delight can blend." *The Art of Poetry. An Epistle to the Pisos. Project Gutenberg*. 5 October 2014. https://www.gutenberg.org/cache/epub/9175/pg9175-images.html. Accessed 25 July 2024.

"Index to the Works of Angela Thirkell by Hazel Bell, Adapted by Suzanne Williams." https://angelathirkellsociety.org/writings/index/. Accessed 9 July 2024.

"John Henry Lorimer." *Wikipedia*. Wikimedia Foundation, Inc. 16 August 2023. https://en.wikipedia.org/wiki/John_Henry_Lorimer. Accessed 12 August 2024.

Newman, John Henry. "Knowledge is its own reward." *The Idea of a University Defined and Illustrated. Project Gutenberg EBook*. 5 February 2008. https://www.gutenberg.org/cache/epub/24526/pg24526-images.html. Accessed 22 July 2024.

Roberts, Adam. "Walter Scott Woodstock 1826." May 28,2022. https://medium.com/adams-notebook/walter-scott-woodstock-1826-47fcbeba0366. Accessed 25 June 2024.

Scott, Sir Walter. *Woodstock.*1855. *Project Gutenberg.* 1 Jan 2006/ 26 June 2021. https://www.gutenberg.org/cache/epub/9785/pg9785-images.html . Accessed 8 July 2024.

Shopify Staff. "How Does Product Placement Work? Examples and Benefits." 12 July 2023. https://www.shopify.com/blog/product-placement   Accessed 8 July 2024.

Strickland, Margot. *Anglela Thirkell: Portrait of a Lady Novelist.* London: Duckworth. 1977.

Temple, Hilary. "*Summer Half* (1937) by Angela Thirkell." 30 July 2019. https://reading19001950.wordpress.com/2019/07/30/summer-half-1937-by-angela-thirkell/ Accessed 27 June 2024.

Thirkell, Angela. Introduction. *The Warden.* By Anthony Trollope. NY: The Heritage Press, 1955. ix-xviii.

---. *Love among the Ruins.* New York: Knopf, 1948.

---. *Love at All Ages.* New York: Knopf, 1959.

--- *Summer Half.* London: The Hogarth Press, 1988.

Virgil. "Love conquers all things." *Eclogue X. The Bucolics and Eclogues. Project Gutenberg.* 10 March 2008. https://www.gutenberg.org/files/230/230-h/230-h.htm. Accessed 25 July 2024.

"'What books are on your nightstand?' Ketanji Brown Jackson." By the Book in *The New York Times Book Review.* 15 September 2024. p.5.

Foreigners in Barsetshire: An Introduction

By Penelope Fritzer

Penelope Fritzer is the Angela Thirkell Society of North America's chair, a retired Florida Atlantic University professor emeritus, and an author.

Several themes run throughout Angela Thirkell's Barsetshire novels, one of them being ethnicity. The novels all take place in England and laud the rural past and the upper middle and upper classes as representing what Orville Prescott calls "enduring British virtue" (2). But it is important as we look at the treatment of foreigners in the books to note L.A.G. Strong's remark that "[Angela Thirkell] is one of the subtlest social historians, in that the reader can seldom be quite sure which of the county values she endorses and which she is laughing at" (250). Strong's is a comment that must be remembered when reading about Barsetshire, as to read with enjoyment, one must put aside political agendas, firmly grasp the historical context, and empty one's mind of modern indignation and political correctness. With those disclaimers out of the way, one can examine the humorous elements of Thirkell's characters' views of foreigners, most used for comic effect and based on stereotypes of the time. Thirkell mocks the English as well: in response to some unflattering photographs of her, she writes, "I am obviously Being English, with my coat drooping at the back," so sometimes her humor raises admiration that an Englishwoman could so laugh at her own "with mixed affection and amusement" (qtd. in Strickland 160 and 171).

Not many non-English characters appear in the early books, and throughout, the ones who do are nearly all caricatures, from the arrogant French to the oblivious Americans. The early novels have fewer references to foreigners than do the later ones, obviously because foreigners played a smaller role in English life in the 1930s than during and after the war years, and the references in the earlier books are lighter-hearted, rather marveling neutrally at their odd habits than actually seeming to dislike them.

The war and post-war novels contain many more views of foreigners, as the general upheaval of society resulted in an unprecedented mixing of diverse nationalities. *The Times* [London] says of the books of this period, "Fortunately, Mrs. Thirkell has no false shame and rather glories in her prejudices" [or, rather, the humorous prejudices of her characters] (449). Hermione Lee refers to Thirkell's "enthusiasm for her characters' swipes at foreigners . . . increas[ing] in frequency during and after the war years" (93), but, again, it is important to realize that Thirkell is a sophisticated enough author to use many of the truculently humorous remarks of the English as much to point up their own provincial outlook as actually to comment on foreigners.

During the coronation summer of Queen Elizabeth in 1953, eight years after the end of the war, Dean Crawley "(quite rightly, we feel) . . . refus[ed] to have representatives of Russia, Japan, Persia, Egypt, and Communism included in the great Tableau of All Nations" (*What Did It Mean?* 9). Even the lower classes are somewhat aware of world politicians, as Effie Bunce says her bossy father "'seems to think he's old Staylin, he does'" (133), while in Close Quarters, Mrs. Macfadyen's cook remarks on "old Nasser and old Cruskoff—whom Mr. Wickham privately identified as one of the nastier Russians—and all them Syprots" (57).

A crowd at a bus stop gets restless when most are left behind by a crowded bus: "[F]oreigners, that's what it was . . . might as well be in Russia . . . I'd tell old Staylin what I thought of him if I was them" (*The Old Bank House* 351). In the same book, Mrs. Morland discusses, with the fine insouciance of the island dweller:

> "[H]ow silly we are to encourage foreigners. I mean Mazzini using the British Museum Reading Room *free*, just like Karl Marx, and then they all turn round and bite us. Look how we let the Mixo-Lydian refugees be here in the war and what do we get for it? They say we are devils and Tony [her son in government service] has to work seventeen hours a day and all his weekends about their dreadful boundaries. I cannot *think* . . . why foreigners always want boundaries. I suppose it comes of not knowing geography" (230-31).

County Chronicle has Nurse showing similar insularity: "'Foreigners in the kitchen . . . and the family taking up with all sorts of people'" (94), while in *A Double Affair*, Dean Crawley:

> bemoans the East: Trouble in the Near East as usual, or Middle East, one never knew which was which. Drat those small nations, he said, who could not keep their hands from picking and stealing and coveting their neighbor's canal or his pipe line or anything that was his. Some of those toy nations, he said, could never be happy unless they were coveting their neighbor's ox and his ass (250).

The above is a very amusing passage, given England's world empire, which was breaking up in 1957 when *A Double Affair* was written. There were problems with Egypt, Cyprus, the Suez Canal, and between Israel and the Arab states, at least partly as a result of the British earlier handing the problem to the United Nations as well as having acted with France and Israel in a failed attempt to take over the canal in 1956.

Similarly, 1958's *Close Quarters* describes the talk at a dinner party as covering "the complete horribleness of practically all Africa and Asia, most of Europe, and large parts of the Americas; pride of place in horribleness being of course awarded to the Middle East" (49). Insular as these reminiscences are, Thirkell tops them with Mr. Halliday's remark in *Enter Sir Robert*:

> I blame Genghis Khan for a good deal. . . [h]e conquered pretty well all northern Asia, and then he tried for Japan, but there were storms and he lost nearly all his ships and a lot of his men, and he had to come back. If I had been there with a few British troops we'd have shown them! (244).

Such descriptions underscore Thirkell's delight in the inside joke of making even her admirable characters look smug and narrow-minded. In the same vein, she describes a fine meal served at the local inn, "And very good it was. Not imaginative; we will leave that to foreigners" by a waiter who points out that the Ritz is "'quite good class but [does] get some queer guests, foreigners and that like'" (*A Double Affair* 240).

Jutland Cottage contains a rousing discussion of kings, even down to the question of Divine Right, during which Mary Leslie dismisses various examples simply with,

"'[T]hey are all foreigners and have revolutions'" (29), harkening back to England's relative stability during the 1800s, in which it was one of the few areas of western Europe without revolution, but in a fine example of Thirkell's use of irony, ignoring the English Civil War of the 1600s.

Even so slight a topic as crossword puzzles can bring on the insular fever:

> "[T]he English Cross-Word . . . we find the best of any we have met. As for French and German ones they are still and always will be in the Kindergarten stage. Of Russia (if any) we know nothing for their alphabet is all wrong all over in shape and lettering, and anyway, who wants to do a Russian crossword, probably produced (as all their sports are) on a wholly professional basis and state-aided? The American cross-words are usually too large and do not run true to form. But *The Times, The Thunderer,* somehow produces a classic almost every day" (*Enter Sir Robert* 242).

In book after book of Angela Thirkell's Barsetshire series, it is made abundantly clear that English (not even British, as we shall see in the future) is best. Thirkell writes, "Any foreigner can become a British subject and most of them do, but we who are English were born so and will please ourselves" ("The Advance of Science" 8). There are many other instances of humor throughout the Barsetshire books about specific foreigners, which shall be examined in the coming issues of *Divagations*.

Works Cited

Lee, Hermione. "Good Show: Why Do So Many Readers Seek Refuge in Angela Thirkell's Little England?" *The New Yorker*. 7 October 1996: 90-95.

Prescott, Orville. "Review of *The Headmistress* by Angela Thirkell." *The New York Times* VI 22 January 1945. 15:2.

Strickland, Margot. *Angela Thirkell: Portrait of a Lady Novelist*. London: Gerald Duckworth and Company, 1977. 2nd printing Angela Thirkell Society North American Branch. Kearny Nebraska: Morris Publishing, 1996.

Strong, L. A. G. "Review of *Happy Return* by Angela Thirkell." *The Spectator* 22 August 1952. 189:250.

The Times [London] Literary Supplement. "Review of *Marling Hall* by Angela Thirkell." 12 September 1942: 449.

Thirkell, Angela. "The Advance of Science." qtd. In *The Journal of the Angela Thirkell Society*. No. 11: 8.

Thirkell, Angela. *Close Quarters*. New York: Alfred Knopf, 1958.

Thirkell, Angela. *County Chronicle*. London: Hamish Hamilton, 1950.

Thirkell, Angela. *A Double Affair*. London: Hamish Hamilton, 1957.

Thirkell, Angela. *Enter Sir Robert*. New York: Alfred Knopf, 1955.

Thirkell, Angela. *Jutland Cottage*. London: Hamish Hamilton, 1953.

Thirkell, Angela. *The Old Bank House*. London: Hamish Hamilton, 1949.

Thirkell, Angela. *What Did It Mean?* London: Hamish Hamilton, 1954.

A Third Dues Reminder

Please don't forget to pay your Angela Thirkell Society of North America dues and maybe give a gift membership or make a donation. All greatly appreciated.

Please send $15 for each membership to treasurer Melanie Osterman at Angela Thirkell Society, PO Box 80133, Lansing, MI 48908-0133.

Lydia and Rose and Shakespeare

By Norma Munson

Our new member chair finds something new to relate to and to smile about with each re-reading of Thirkell's novels.

When thinking about favorite humorous scenes in Thirkell novels, one that comes to mind involves Lydia, Rose, and Shakespeare.

In Hazel Bell's "Index to the writings of Angela Thirkell," there are more than 25 entries for Shakespeare with multiple references under those, helping to reveal how steeped Thirkell was in Shakespeare, and how frequently she brings him into the novels via various characters as well as unattributed allusions.

In *Summer Half,* two favorite characters, Lydia Keith and Rose Birkett, are portrayed as having definite opinions and sometimes humorous reactions to Shakespeare. In Chapter IV, Lydia takes the train to London to meet Noel Merton at the Old Vic to see a production of *Othello.* Noel observes that Lydia seemed to hold her breath in a trance at the rise of the curtain and not breathe again until the interval. After a pause to let her come up for air, he asks if she would like to walk a bit, so they go into the foyer. Lydia enthuses that "'everything he [Shakespeare] says seems to have something to do with oneself.'" She thinks he "'must have had an extraordinary mind. I mean he has such a wonderful vocabulary'" (83,84).

Lydia has already formed her opinion that although some of Shakespeare's vocabulary is beyond her, she usually doesn't look up the words because she believes he expected people to know them and if people didn't, he didn't mind. She comments on the tragic aspects of the play but ends her comments with, "'But somehow when it's Shakespeare it's all right.'" (84)

On the other hand, Rose Birkett in Chapter VI has a quite different understanding of Shakespeare. She is having a flirtatious exchange with Noel during tea at the annual Southbridge school sports day. She politely asks him if he has seen any shows lately. What follows is a hilarious dialogue revealing her misunderstandings about the plays, the characters, and the actors. "It had gradually become obvious to everyone that Rose thought there was a play called alternatively Shakespeare and Hamlet. No one felt equal to explaining this." (141-2) The reader has to smile at this last line of the paragraph.

Lydia enters the fray, giving a short tutoring session to Rose: "'I know what's wrong with you...you don't read enough....after all Shakespeare was not for an age but for all time'" (142). Her passionate opinions even impress Tony Morland and Noel, and, eventually, the topic expands to classical literature.

Soon the group drifts apart to various activities, and Colin takes pity on Rose and diverts her by asking her to help him clear away the tea things and prepare for more guests. The topic of Shakespeare is forgotten.

Scenes like this confirm our impressions of the personalities of the characters and reveal new insights with each chapter. There is no end to the enjoyment of recalling favorite scenes in Thirkell novels.

Work Cited

Thirkell, Angela. *Summer Half.* London: The Hogarth Press, 1988.

Modestine and Other Donkeys

By Susan Verell, a huge fan of all things equine

How did Angela Thirkell gain her insights into donkey behavior? She seemed to understand Modestine and make him come to life for her readers. Although Angela Thirkell lived mostly in cities, she must have encountered and been interested in the rural-based animals that appear in her books.

Angela's insights are worth examining. She reveals much about Modestine from her narrative as well as from his dialogue with the Tebbens' cat, Gunnar. People who know donkeys understand that they are social animals who depend on friendships to add to their enjoyment of life. How lonely Modestine would have been without Gunnar. They begin their conversations with gossip, Gunnar picking up tidbits from observing and from discussions with the Deans' cat, Kitty. The conversations then wander into the discussion of food and drink. Modestine is a vegetarian who thinks that is the best life choice for Gunnar and reminds Gunnar of his disgusting eating habits. Gunnar calls Modestine an ignorant and mad vegetarian. Modestine appears to frown on Gunnar's drinking habits, as Gunnar consumes both sherry and enough alcohol to give him a hangover, points of discussion in two separate dialogues in *August Folly.*

Modestine is discerning regarding his human acquaintances, so his uncooperative nature is evident only with the people he dislikes. Much of his hostility toward members of the Tebben family revolves around the donkey cart, also referred to as the little governess cart, which Modestine hates. In a display of temper, Modestine tells Gunnar that he wants to destroy the cart, toss Mrs. Tebben over the hedge, stomp on Mr. Tebben, and then go and join the army (178). Modestine is fond of Jessica Dean because she gives him sugar. He also cooperates with Bert Margett, the railway porter, and with Jessica's Nanny. Modestine prefers to do as both these people instruct him to do, rather than to listen to any of the Tebben family's pleas.

Donkeys also prefer meaningful work. Mr. Tebben announces that he hates Modestine, and Richard Tebben calls Modestine a lazy brute, because of their ignorance of the donkey's personality. Angela Thirkell uses the condemnation of Modestine to illustrate character issues in the humans who make disparaging remarks. Mules have worked for years at the National Parks throughout the United States. Mules inherit their strong work ethic from their donkey fathers (mules are hybrids, bred from a female horse and a male donkey). One park ranger who worked with mules told me that the worst part of his day was going to the stable and harnessing five mules for a long day at work and leaving three mules in their stalls because the mules left behind were mournful and made him feel very guilty.

Another personality trait of donkeys that Angela Thirkell understands is their fear of the unknown. Donkeys are intelligent, and many of their fears appear to stem from their ability to consider possibilities. When Nanny and Jessica Dean first meet Modestine, he stops dead, "in affected terror at the sight of a small stone" (85). The stone is an unknown. It could have been an explosive or an egg of a creature that could hurt Modestine. The possibilities were there. It was just good donkey logic to stop and consider them all.

After the incident in *August Folly* where Richard Tebben is credited with saving Jessica Dean from the bull Rushwater Rubicon, Richard shows an improvement in his personality by giving Modestine a moment of glory as the savior in the situation during a conversation with Mr. Fanshawe. After all, Modestine did cooperate with Richard, a rarity, and let

45

Richard lead him to block the path of the bull. Modestine also held the bull's stare and bared his teeth, leading Rushwater Rubicon to seek out the cowman who was trying to catch him. The hero of the day is Modestine, yet Richard benefited a great deal from the incident.

No article about Modestine should omit the history behind his name. Richard was distressed to learn from Susan Dean that Modestine is named for Robert Louis Stevenson's donkey Modestine described in *Travels with a Donkey in the Cevennes.* "Of all the affected, ridiculous names that an elderly he-donkey could be called, Modestine was the worst" (87).

Also, clarification is needed about the name Modestine and the name Neddy. The donkey didn't have a name change. The term Neddy is British slang, especially used by children, to refer to a donkey, according to Dictionary.com. Mrs. Tebben names her donkey Modestine. Characters including Bert Margett, Nanny, and the Dean family call Modestine Neddy despite being corrected by members of the Tebben family. A similar habit is calling a cat Kitty instead of by the name given to the cat by its owners.

August Folly concludes with Modestine telling Gunnar that he wishes for retirement, doing light work and taking Jessica Dean for rides; there would be no more station work with the donkey cart. Modestine gets his wish, as explained by Susan Dean to Richard Tebben in *Love Among the Ruins.* "Your mother sold him to my mother, and he was useful in the garden and about the farm. Then the war came, and we sold him to an evacuated nursery school. I believe he is still alive'" (79). It all sounds like an appropriate and well-deserved life of leisure.

In closing, one more example of Angela Thirkell's respect for the donkey is worth noting. In the last conversation with Gunnar, cited in *August Folly*, Modestine hums a few bars of "Non-Piu Andrai" from Mozart's *The Marriage of Figaro*

(288). Anyone showcasing his opera knowledge ranks high with Mrs. Thirkell. Gunnar is not a fan, as he is suffering from a hangover and prefers silence.

Works Cited

Thirkell, Angela. *August Folly.* New York: Carroll & Graff Publishers, Inc., 1995.

Thirkell, Angela. *Love Among the Ruins.* London: Hamish Hamilton, 1948.

Thirkell Society member Norma Munson has a donkey named Otis (pictured at left) as a neighbor. Do you have a donkey friend? Please send a photo for the next issue.

Married Couples Crossword

Across:
- 3. Alured Bond
- 5. Lucasta Bond
- 6. Millie Pollett
- 8. Kate Carter
- 11. Harold Downing
- 12. Charles Belton
- 14. Aubrey Clover
- 19. Susan Barton
- 22. Sam Adams

Down:
- 1. George Halliday
- 2. Freddie Belton
- 4. Lucy Adams
- 7. Cedric Bond
- 9. Francis Crofts
- 10. Ted Pilward
- 13. Adrian Coates
- 14. Rose Fairweather
- 15. Madeline Carton
- 16. Jeffery Palliser
- 17. Sybil Coates
- 18. Daphne Bond
- 20. William Birkett
- 21. Lettice Barclay

Sightings

Sheila Pim (1909-1995) was an Irish writer who wrote a biography of the Irish plant collector Augustine Henry, three non-fiction books about gardening, three novels of Irish life, and four Irish Village Mysteries in the 1950s and 60s (which were reprinted in the early 2000s by Rue Morgue Press). The reprints each open with a page about the author and note that all the novels "had some mystery elements but were primarily novels of Irish life, prompting some reviewers to describe her as the Irish Angela Thirkell. Gardening was a key element in all of her books."

From Penelope Fritzer

In the July 2024, No. 27, issue of *The Scribbler: A Retrospective Literary Review,* there is a four-page article about Angela Thirkell's Laura Morland in the section titled "Reviews--Fictional Authors." The writer Sally Phillips compares Mrs. Laura Morland to Agatha Christie's *alter ego* Ariadne Oliver and goes on from there to give an account of Mrs. Morland as she appears through time in Thirkell's novels. She concludes that Laura Morland has not changed very much over the years and that as she approached 70 years old, "...all the great and good of Barsetshire are proud to consider her a friend, and it is not surprising that she is one of Thirkell's most popular characters."

The other authors with their *alter egos* in the section are O. Douglas's 'Merren Strang," Joanna Cannan's 'Alison Dunbar,' and Elsie Oxenham's 'Mary-Dorothy Devine.'

From Norma Munson

From Alan Bradley's *The Grave's a Fine Private Place,* Delacorte: 2018, page 145.

"'The spell for finding books," [Daffy] whispered, closing her eyes before pronouncing the incantation: "'Abracadabra, Alakazam, Angela Thirkell, Omar Khayyam." I had never seen my sister so excited."

[This is a Flavia de Luce novel – a murder mystery. Flavia is a 12-year-old sleuth.]

From John Childery

My friend Christine Shuttleworth was reading Joan Wyndham's autobiography *Anything Once* and emailed this bit to me:

"More brilliant people arrived after dinner, like Stephen Spender and Peter Quennell, and everybody was being terribly bitchy about everyone else. It was like being in a nest of intellectual vipers. Nice Angela Thirkell was referred to as 'Arsenic and Old Lace,' and everybody seemed to loathe poor [Arthur] Koestler, and called him a phony communist. As for Connolly, he was known as 'Squirrel.'"

From Norma Munson

A donkey sighting to accompany the Modestine article in this issue: In *Jutland Cottage* (1953), page 258, I found a quote to use as a reminder that Angela Thirkell never forgot donkeys. Rose Fairweather says, "'John and I are going down to join the children near Bognor next week. They are having a splendid time. There are tennis tournaments for under-twelves and lovely sands and even donkeys.'"

They must have been on Angela Thirkell's mind, as she writes on page 260 that, as Mr. Wickham says to Canon

Fewling and Miss Phelps: "'Well, here's to Horatio Nelson coupled with the name of–what the hell *is* your name, Tubby? I've known you for donkey's ears, but we always said Tubby.'"

He answers, "'I can't help it, but it's George.'"

From Barbara Houlton

From *A Bite of the Apple; A Life with Books, Writers, and Virago* by Lennie Goodings, Oxford University Press, 2020:

Page 83— "Unsurprisingly, Carmen [Callil, publisher of Virago Cooperative] developed the Australian Classics: Miles Franklin, Angela Thirkell, Henry Handel Richardson, Christina Stead, and later Shirley Hazzard...."

From Norma Munson

I just read Robert Harris' new novel *Precipice*-- a historical story about the romance between British Prime Minister H.H. Asquith and socialite Venetia Stanley during World War I and found a Thirkell connection in it, without mentioning Thirkell's name:

"She had left the following afternoon and travelled by car to Stanway House in Gloucestershire for another party, given by Lord and Lady Wemyss, whose daughter, Cynthia, was married to Beb Asquith."

From Jay Strafford

Tidbits and Glimpses and Sightings

From Sara Bowen

The quotes are from The Afterlife: Essays and Criticism by Penelope Fitzgerald, edited by Terence Dooley, published by Counterpoint: New York, 2003. Fitzgerald died in 2000, and this was edited posthumously.

p. 86. Fitzgerald quotes Jane Morris's comment on Mackail's Life of William Morris: "'You see, Mackail [Angela Thirkell's father] is not an artist in feeling, and therefore cannot be sympathetic while writing the life of such a man.'"

Fitzgerald gave a lecture at the Annual General Meeting of the William Morris Society in 1994, which she then published in 1998 in The Journal of the William Morris Society. The following items are from that talk.

On page 313, Rudyard Kipling spent his Christmas holidays at the Grange in the 1870s after his parents went back to India. Fitzgerald notes that he wrote about this respite from his misery in Something of Myself.

"Here he had love and affection, he says, 'as much as the greediest could desire' – and he was not very greedy -- the smell of paint and turpentine, and in the rooms 'chairs and cupboards such as the world had not yet seen, for our Deputy Uncle Topsy was just beginning to fabricate these things.' And once when little Ruddie and Margaret [Angela Thirkell's mother] were eating bread and dripping in the nursery, Morris came in and sat on the rocking horse and 'slowly surging back and forth while the poor beast creaked, he told us a tale full of fascinating horrors, about a man who was condemned to dream bad dreams….He went away as abruptly as he had come. Long afterwards, when I was old enough to know a maker's pains, it dawned on me that we must have heard the Saga of Burnt Njal.'"

On page 318, Fitzgerald describes the last relic of The Grange:

"In *Three Houses*, The Grange appears as a children's paradise even more paradisal than it had been to Rudyard Kipling in the 1870s, partly because while Kipling was understood and most kindly treated, Angela was grossly spoiled. When she was born Burne-Jones entered on yet another term of hopeless slavery. He was in a state of open rivalry with Gladstone as to which of them could spoil their granddaughters the most. Angela always sat next to him at lunch, blew the froth off his beer, had her bread buttered on both sides, rushed into the kitchen to talk to Robert the parrot. The children were free to roam the whole house, except the studio, and yet she saw William Morris only once, in Georgie's sitting room. She saw him as 'an old man (or so I thought him) with the aggressive mop of white hair who was talking, between fits of coughing, to my grandmother.'"

"The Grange is now 'a house of air.' But when Georgie went to live permanently in Rottingdean, it must in any case have lost its character. Kipling certainly thought so when he wrote about 'the open-work iron bell-pull on the wonderful gate that let me into all felicity. When I had a house of my own, and The Grange was emptied of meaning, I begged for and was given the bell-pull for my entrance, in the hope that other children might also feel happy when they rang it.' It is all that is left, but it means that anyone who goes to Batemans can feel they have at least been in touch with The Grange."

Crossword Puzzle Key

Special thanks to Melanie Osterman for the crossword puzzle and key!

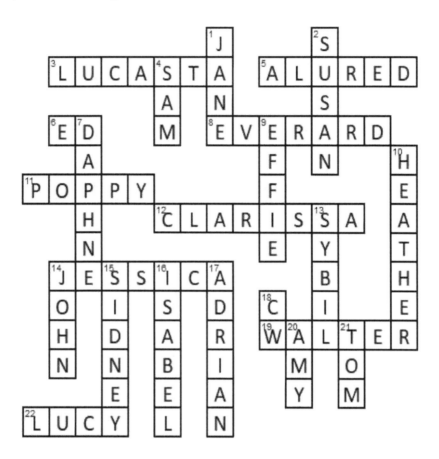

Angela Thirkell Titles

*1931 Three Houses
*1933 Ankle Deep
 1933 High Rising
 1934 Wild Strawberries
*1934 Trooper to the Southern Cross
 1934 The Demon in the House
*1935 Oh, These Men, These Men!
*1935 The Grateful Sparrow
*1936 The Fortunes of Harriette
 1936 August Folly
*1937 Coronation Summer
 1937 Summer Half
 1938 Pomfret Towers
 1939 The Brandons
 1939 Before Lunch
 1940 Cheerfulness Breaks In
 1941 Northbridge Rectory
 1942 Marling Hall
 1943 Growing Up
 1944 The Headmistress
 1945 Miss Bunting
 1946 Peace Breaks Out
 1947 Private Enterprise
 1948 Love Among the Ruins
 1949 The Old Bank House
 1950 County Chronicle
 1951 The Duke's Daughter
 1952 Happy Return
 1953 Jutland Cottage
 1954 What Did It Mean?
 1955 Enter Sir Robert
 1956 Never Too Late
 1957 A Double Affair
 1958 Close Quarters
 1959 Love at All Ages
 1961 Three Score and Ten

* Denotes a book not set in Barsetshire

Contacts

Angela Thirkell Society of North America: PO Box 80133, Lansing, MI 48908, www.angelathirkellsociety.org, barsetshireATS@gmail.com

Chair: Penelope Fritzer, Periwinkle Cottage, 2610 N.E. 13th Court, Ft. Lauderdale, FL 33304, 954-736-6524, pfritzer@gmail.com.

Treasurer: Melanie Osterman, PO Box 80133, Lansing, MI 48908, ATStreasurer@outlook.com.

Secretary: Suzanne Williams, 759 Maury River Road, Lexington, VA 24450-3401, 207-730-0060, sfw4514@gmail.com.

Vice Chair & Editor: Susan Verell, 801 Betz Creek Rd., Savannah, GA 31410, 912-201-3066, bverell@comcast.net.

Agent for Service: Barbara Houlton, sdhoulton@cox.net.

Academic Coordinator: John Childrey, 11055 NW 38th St., Coral Springs, FL 33065, 954-257-8848, Childrey@fau.edu

New Members: Norma Munson, 5225 Ponderosa Drive, Rockford, IL 61107, 815-877-3530, nkmuson62@comcast.net.

Publications & Books: Jerri Chase, P.O. Box 234, Kingston, AR 72742-0234, 479-665-2340, danjerri@madisoncounty.net.

Website: Susannah Smith, subukastawa@gmail.com

Public Relations: Tom Johnson, 581 Eldora Road, Pasadena, CA 91104-3614, 626-797-8289, maxdaddytj@yahoo.com.

Original Art: Deborah Conn, Deborahconn@verizon.net.

Cover Production: Diane Smook, Dpsmook@earthlink.net.